The Queen Elizabeth Coronation Book

By
NEIL FERRIER

MCMLIII

Her Majesty's quick grasp of affairs of State is largely owing to the careful training given her by her father.
A photograph taken at Royal Lodge, Windsor in 1942.

A family group taken in one of the State Rooms of Windsor Castle in February 1944.

An Elder Brother of Trinity House.
A recent photograph by Baron of H.R.H. the Duke of Edinburgh.

Photo : Baron

H.R.H. the Princess Elizabeth and H.R.H. the Duke of Edinburgh after their wedding in 1947.

ST. EDWARD'S CROWN.

Since 1661, when it was made for Charles II by Sir Robert Vyner, the Court Jeweller, the Kings and Queens of England have been crowned with this magnificent symbol of sovereignty.   Made of solid gold it is set with precious stones.   The purple velvet Cap of Maintenance inside is edged with ermine.

Foreword

It was on her twenty-first birthday that, in a broadcast speech to the Commonwealth, Queen Elizabeth said, " I declare before you all that my whole life, whether it be long or short, shall be devoted to your service and the service of the great Imperial family to which we all belong." Then she went on to say, " But I shall not have strength to carry out this resolution alone unless you join in it with me, as I now invite you to do ; I know that your support will be unfailingly given." Her Coronation will be for the Queen a time of re-dedication ; for her people it can be a chance to show by the sincerity and warmth of their rejoicing that the support she asked for is indeed hers and will not fail her.

The Coronation of an English Sovereign is at once an awe-inspiring reality and a symbol. The reality is that of the might and wealth of a great Union of Free Nations displayed in all its magnificence to pay tribute to the power that binds them together. The symbol is the dedication of this power, embodied in the single person of the Sovereign, to the service of God.

In the rites that celebrate this dedication there is much of the English character to be seen ; a love of pageantry, a veneration for tradition that allows of compromise, a very real and profound religious awe. This is a most special ceremony, yet its strength lies in the mixture within it of what is awe-inspiring and novel with what is simple and familiar.

Only once or twice in a lifetime can an Englishman expect to witness a Coronation, therefore the ceremonies connected with it are bound to seem a little strange to most observers. Yet this unique and complicated ceremonial is embedded in and made part of a Holy Communion Service such as takes place regularly in every village church throughout the land. Even those parts of the service which seem strangest are familiar enough in outline to those who have ever witnessed the installation of a Bishop, and it is fitting that there should be this similarity, for the Sovereign in accepting power is, in the Christian tradition, also accepting a trust.

That Queen Elizabeth truly understands this, no-one has doubted or can doubt, since in her own words and of her own free will, she made that first dedication of her life to her peoples everywhere.

This group of Crown regalia shows the Sovereign's Orb which is placed in the Queen's right hand during the Coronation ceremony. The Crown is again St. Edward's Crown. Next to the Crown is the Sceptre

8

with the Cross and in the foreground the Sceptre with the Dove symbolising the Holy Ghost. The ring is the Sovereign's Ring with the Cross of St. George in sapphires and rubies.

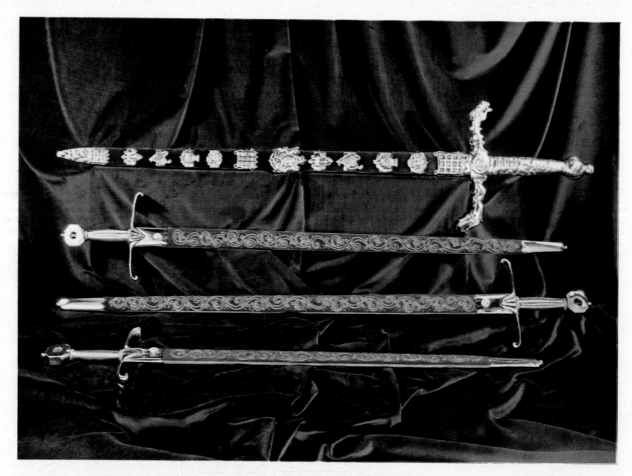

The Swords are (top to bottom) the Sword of State, which is also borne before the Queen at the State Opening of Parliament (see page 72), the Sword of Spiritual Justice, the Sword of Temporal Justice and the Sword of Mercy (Curtana) with its blade broken near the bottom to symbolise mercy.

The Coronation

The date of Queen Elizabeth's Coronation is to be June the second, but much work has to be done before the day arrives. In this the chief parts are played by the Coronation Joint Committee, a body composed largely of high placed Civil Servants and dealing with much of the detail planning, and the Coronation Committee of the Privy Council which decides on the broad lines of policy. Both the Prime Minister and the Leader of Her Majesty's Opposition are members of the latter body and the Duke of Edinburgh is its Chairman. Serving on both these committees, and President of the Joint Committee, is the Earl Marshal, the Duke of Norfolk, who may be said to be in charge of all secular arrangements for the occasion.

Many and complicated are the points that must be settled, ranging from decisions on what parts of the service are to be televised to the timing of processions and the ordering of precedence among visiting foreign representatives. Much advice also has to be made available for local authorities outside the capital who wish to mark the day with their own celebrations.

As the day approaches the actual preparations begin. For many months Westminster Abbey is closed while the interior is built up with tiered stands of seats to accommodate over seven thousand people. The Court of Claims sits to decide who is qualified by hereditary right to take an active part in the service, like, for instance, the Lord of the Manor of Worksop who is entitled to stand near the Queen during the ceremony and support her right arm if it should tire under the weight of the sceptre. During this time too, buildings fronting the streets through which the processions will pass are freshly cleaned and painted, stands are erected and supports arranged to bear flags and decorations. There is also a brisk demand for tickets, and accommodation for the day may, as at the Coronation of King George the Sixth, cost as much as £25. Still nearer the time the processions are rehearsed, usually at an hour when there will be little or no traffic on the roads.

On the Coronation day, while the great processions are assembling, the Regalia, which have been brought from their permanent home in the Tower of London, are being handed by the clergy of Westminster Abbey to those high officers of state who are to bear them during the ceremony. Outside the crowds wait, as many of them have waited all night, for the appearance of the Queen.

Then the processions begin to pass along the route. Four main elements contribute to this magnificent spectacle. First there is the Lord Mayor's Procession typifying commerce and the material wealth on which the country's prosperity is based. Then follow the representatives of foreign countries who have come to do honour to the Queen. Thirdly comes our own Parliamentary Leader, the Prime Minister, representing the Government of the country and followed by the Prime Ministers of the Dominions and the Rulers and Representatives of the Colonies. And finally there pass the processions of the various members of the Royal Family culminating in the procession of the Queen. The forces of the Crown are of

The Sceptre with the Cross has the largest cut diamond in the world mounted in its head. It is the Great Star of Africa cut from the famous Cullinan Diamond. The diamond is worn on State occasions as a pendant and is detached by removing the four gold clasps which hold it.

The Great State Coach which will be used to convey Queen Elizabeth to and from Westminster Abbey is here seen receiving an overhaul in the Royal Mews of Buckingham Palace. It is used only at Coronations.

Part of the Sovereign's escort of the Blues (Royal Horse Guards) waiting to escort Princess Elizabeth and the Duke of Edinburgh to Buckingham Palace after the Royal wedding in November 1947. The Household Cavalry will play a major part in the ceremonial after the Coronation, it being their privilege and duty to attend the State Coach in the procession.

course represented by mounted escorts for the Royal processions and by the aides-de-camp and top ranking officers of the three Services who precede the Queen. There is also a special escort for Her Majesty consisting of British, Dominion and Colonial troops, and the great state coach in which she makes the journey is followed by the Princes of the Blood and the Queen's suite.

At the Abbey those people who have travelled in the earlier processions take their places to await the Queen's arrival and the clergy and bearers of the Regalia are now stationed at the west door to receive Her Majesty and conduct her up the Nave to the Sanctuary. The procession is a magnificent one, the Abbey clergy and Arch-bishops of Canterbury and York leading with

great officers of state, and the highest dignitaries of the realm carrying the Regalia, followed by three Bishops, then the Queen herself clad in a crimson robe of state. On either side of her walk the Bishop of Durham and the Bishop of Bath and Wells, and eight pages carry her train. A body-guard of Gentlemen-at-Arms accompanies her and after members of the Queen's household and others the Yeomen of the Guard bring up the rear. An anthem is sung as the procession passes and as the Queen comes level with the Choir the Queen's scholars of Westminster School greet her with their traditional cry of " Vivat, Regina Elizabetha, vivat, vivat, vivat."

In the Sanctuary the Queen prays for a few moments as a private individual before moving to

One of the oldest items of the Regalia still in use at Coronation ceremonies is the Ampulla, an eagle-shaped container for the anointing oil. With it in the picture is the beautifully decorated spoon into which the oil is poured before the anointing takes place.

her chair of state on the south side of the open space called the Theatre, then the first stage of the Coronation ceremony begins. This is called the Recognition and is the formal presentation of the Sovereign to her people so that they may show by acclamation their wish that she and no other shall reign over them.

The Queen stands and the Archbishop of Canterbury, Lord Chancellor, Lord Great Chamberlain and Lord High Constable, all preceded by the Garter King at Arms, walk to the east side of the Theatre. The Archbishop then addresses the people saying " Sirs, I here present unto you Queen Elizabeth, your undoubted

Queen : wherefore all you who are come this day to do your homage and service, are you willing to do the same ? " The response is a loud and repeated cry of " God save Queen Elizabeth." This challenge and answer being repeated on each of the other three sides of the Theatre, the Queen facing each in turn, the Recognition is completed by the sounding of trumpets.

At this point all the items of the Regalia are handed over by their bearers to the Dean of Westminster who lays them on the altar.

The next part of the ceremony is the taking of the Coronation Oath which is administered to the Queen by the Archbishop. This oath is in several parts to each of which the Queen must give her assent, promising to rule her peoples according to the laws and customs of their separate countries and to maintain the Laws of God, the Protestant Religion and the Church of England of which, as Queen, she is the head. Finally, kneeling at the altar steps and with her right hand on the Holy Gospel she seals her solemn oath with the words " The things which I have here before promised, I will perform and keep. So help me God." She then kisses the Book and signs a copy of the Oath in permanent witness of what she has just undertaken. The sacred Oath signed, the Queen then returns to her Chair of State. Had she not already done so at the opening of Parliament last November, this is the point at which the Queen would repeat the Statutory Declaration of her belief in and support of the Protestant Faith.

Being now accepted by her subjects, and having sworn to rule them according to Law Divine and Human, the Queen is ready for the culminating stages of her progress to absolute sovereignty, the Anointing and the Coronation.

Both these acts have a profound mystical significance and it is hard to say which is the more ancient. Certainly the Kings of Israel are described

The magnificence and majesty of earthly rule are symbolized in the Imperial State Crown with its 3,093 jewels which include the Black Prince's ruby, worn by King Henry V at Agincourt ; the Star of Africa, part of the fabulous Cullinan diamond ; and in the centre of the upper cross a sapphire said to have come from King Edward the Confessor's ring.

Westminster Abbey, scene of the Coronation of all but two of England's Kings and Queens in the last 900 years.

A historic moment.   The Archbishop of Canterbury places the Crown on the head of King George VI.

A study of Their Royal Highnesses taken in the Drawing Room at Clarence House in 1951. The blue gown was one of Her Majesty's favourite dresses.

Photo : Baron

Prince Charles sees something to amuse him on his second birthday, 14th November 1950.

as being anointed in Old Testament times, while the idea of Coronation probably came from the specially valuable or ornate helmet worn by tribal leaders in ancient times to denote their authority and act as a rallying point in battle. However from the religious point of view there is no doubt at all that the Anointing is the most important gift the Sovereign receives, for it is by this act that she is given God's authority to rule.

It is therefore in preparation for this solemn event that the Communion Service is now begun, the Queen joining the congregation in prayer and in the singing of that great creed which expresses the Church's beliefs.

After this she kneels while the hymn, " Come Holy Ghost our Souls inspire," is sung. The Archbishop then invokes a blessing on the Queen, at the same time laying his hand upon the Ampulla which, in the form of a gold eagle, holds the specially prepared oil for the Anointing.

Then while an anthem is sung, the Lord Great Chamberlain takes off the Cap of State and the crimson robe which the Queen has worn until now. Assisted by the Lord Great Chamberlain, before whom is carried the Sword of State, the Queen passes to the altar and then takes her seat on King Edward's Chair while four Knights of the Garter hold over her a rich canopy of cloth of gold.

The Dean of Westminster now takes the Ampulla and the golden anointing spoon from the altar and pours a little of the oil from the beak of the Ampulla so that the spoon is ready for the Archbishop to take. The Archbishop then proceeds to anoint the Queen, probably, following the precedent set at Queen Victoria's Coronation, by tracing a cross on the palm of each hand and on the crown of her head only. As he does this last he says these solemn words. " Be thy head anointed with holy oil, as kings, priests and prophets were anointed : and as Solomon was anointed by Zadok the priest and Nathan the prophet, so be you anointed, blessed and consecrated Queen over the Peoples whom the Lord your God hath given you to rule and govern. In the name of the Father, and of the Son, and of the Holy Ghost. Amen."

The Ampulla and spoon are put back on the altar, the Queen kneels at her faldstool and the Archbishop speaks a blessing over her. The great moment of the anointing is at an end and the Queen returns to the King Edward Chair while the four Knights of the Garter hand back the canopy to the Lord Chamberlain.

But now the Queen rises again and retires to St. Edward's Chapel to be robed for her Coronation. First the Colobium Sindonis is put upon her. This is, for a Sovereign Queen, a long full garment of white linen and lace, which reaches to the feet. Next comes the Supertunica, a long close-fitting belted garment of Cloth of Gold. After her return the ceremony now mounts steadily in richness of display through the investiture with the various items of the Regalia to the final placing of the crown upon the Queen's head. But that is not to say that at this point it turns from a religious ceremony to something less, for the items of the Regalia used in the service are few of them without their religious significance.

The golden spurs that the Queen has to touch are the emblems of chivalry, of a code of behaviour in which justice is done and the poor are protected.

The five State Swords each play their part in defining the role of the Sovereign, though only two are used in the ceremony, the great Sword of State and the Sovereign's Jewelled Sword. The Sword of State being too heavy to be worn is handed by its bearer to the Lord Chamberlain who gives him in return the Jewelled Sword. This is placed on the altar by the Archbishop and a prayer is offered up that the sovereign " may not bear it in vain ; but may use it as the minister of God." It is then put in the Queen's hand but, following the precedent set at Queen Victoria's Coronation, it will probably not be girded round her. Another prayer follows in which the Queen is exhorted to " reform what is amiss and confirm what is in good order." At this point the Queen steps forward offering the sword on the altar, thus signifying the submission of her temporal to God's spiritual authority. The sword is then bought back by its bearer for a nominal value of one hundred shillings. The other three swords carried at the Coronation are the Curtana which has a broken blade to denote mercy, the Sword of Spiritual Justice and the Sword of Temporal Justice.

After the sword the Queen is invested with the Armill or stole and the Robe Royal, an ornately worked garment somewhat resembling a Bishop's cope, is put upon her.

The Orb too is given to her with the injunction " when you see this Orb thus set under the Cross, remember that the whole world is subject to the Power and Empire of Christ our Redeemer."

Then follows the presentation of the ring, " ensign of kingly dignity and of defence of the Catholic faith."

Queen Elizabeth seen in her Princess's robes at the time of her father's Coronation.

A glove presented by the Lord of the Manor of Worksop is next put on and the Archbishop places the Sceptre with the Cross in the Queen's right hand and the Sceptre with the Dove in her left, these signifying that she is to rule with justice and mercy.

Finally to the Queen thus visibly endowed with all the symbolic powers of authority comes the confirmation of actual sovereignty with the placing on her head by the Archbishop of St. Edward's Crown as she sits on King Edward's Chair. She has already been anointed to God but at this moment is given the supreme sign of worldly power, and it is now that her subjects acclaim her,

A familiar sight to any visitor to Windsor Castle in Coronation year. A corporal of the Coldstream Guards changes sentries.

the Peers putting on their coronets, the trumpets sounding, the guns on Tower Hill firing a salute and all those in the Abbey crying " God save the Queen."

At this moment too the Queen takes her place in the great succession of English Sovereigns to whom this Crown, and the original on which it was modelled in the time of Charles the Second, have meant Kingship ; for St. Edward's Crown is used at no other time than during the Coronation service.

After receiving the most that man can give of pomp and power it is fitting that the next gift should be the only one which in its simplicity can

rival the magnificence of the Crown. So it is that the Queen is next presented with a Bible, " the most valuable thing that this world affords," as the Archbishop tells her.

It now only remains for the Queen to be brought to the centre of the Theatre and helped to mount her Throne and she is ready to receive the Homage of her people.

As she sits in splendour, wearing the Crown and holding the two Sceptres, Archbishops and Bishops, the Princes of the Blood and the Peers of the Realm come to stand before her and swear fealty. First the Archbishop of Canterbury, kneeling in front of Her Majesty, speaks for the

A view of Windsor Castle from the Great Park. The battlemented walls and towers dwarf the buildings that cluster at the Castle's foot.

Bishops kneeling behind him this oath which they all repeat with him, but inserting their own names and titles instead of his ; " I Geoffrey, Archbishop of Canterbury will be faithful and true, and faith and truth will bear unto you our Sovereign Lady, and your heirs, Kings of Great Britain, Ireland and the British Dominions beyond the seas and Defenders of the Faith. And I will do, and truly acknowledge, the service of the lands which I claim to hold of you, as in right of the Church. So help me God."

Having said these words the Archbishop kisses the Queen's hand. Then the Princes of the Blood Royal kneel down and take off their coronets while their senior member kneels before the Queen and repeats a form of Oath in which he swears to be the Queen's " liege man of life and limb, and of earthly worship." After which all the Princes of the Blood rise and each coming forward touches the Crown as it rests on Her Majesty's head and also kisses her hand. Queen Anne's consort paid homage even before the Archbishop and this precedent may well be followed by the Duke of Edinburgh. There follow the Peers, each order doing homage separately and saying the Oath with its senior representative kneeling at the Queen's feet. First come the Dukes, then the Marquesses, the Earls, the Viscounts and the Barons.

When all is done and the representative of each order has touched the Crown and kissed the Queen's hand, the drums beat, the trumpets sound and the united congregation gives the seal to this homage of clergy and nobility with a cry of

" God save Queen Elizabeth.
Long live Queen Elizabeth.
May the Queen live for ever."

This is the end of the Coronation but the Service of Holy Communion within which it has been framed continues in the normal way except that the Queen presents to the Archbishop the bread and wine which are used. Later she also makes a gift of an altar cloth and an ingot of gold of a pound weight which the Archbishop places on the Altar.

Throughout this part of the service the Queen kneels at the Altar steps and the Sceptres are held by their original bearers while the Lord Great Chamberlain holds the Crown.

When the Archbishops and Bishops and their assistants at the ceremony have made their Communion, the bread and the wine are administered to the Queen. After this she returns to her throne, reassuming the Crown and Sceptres, and the service ends with the singing of the Te Deum " We praise thee O God : we acknowledge thee to be the Lord."

While this is being sung the Queen is attended to St. Edward's Chapel where the St. Edward Crown, the Royal Robe of State and the Sceptre with the Dove are taken from her. In place of these she receives the Imperial State Crown, a robe of purple velvet and the Orb. She now leaves the Abbey by the same door through which she entered, bearing in her right hand the Sceptre with the Cross and in her left the Orb.

Outside the processions set off on the return journey to Buckingham Palace, but this time the cortege is led by a fully representative selection of the troops of Her Majesty's forces from all over the world. With bands playing and colours unfurled the great marching columns move bravely through the packed troop-lined streets. And so the Queen returns in triumph to her home, anointed, crowned, acclaimed, to reign over the Commonwealth, as all her subjects pray, for many peaceful, prosperous and happy years to come.

For a new reign the curtains now divide
To altered dispositions on the stage,
Youth's vowed devotion in the van to guide
On to a new Elizabethan age.

Give comfort, purpose, strength ;
Grant health and hope ;
Lend wisdom scope,
And may we come at length
To know her name a name all time will bless
Because her courage and devotedness
Continued worthy of her heritage.

The Queen gave the first big party of her reign in December 1952 when she entertained the Prime Ministers of the Commonwealth to dinner at Buckingham Palace. She is shown here with Mr. S. G. Holland (New Zealand), Mr. Winston Churchill, Mr. Robert Menzies (Australia) and Mr. St. Laurent (Canada).

The Royal sisters in one of the State Rooms at Buckingham Palace in May 1942.

Beneath the grey walls of ancient Windsor Castle the Queen watches her daughters at their lessons

The Queen's Christmas Broadcast

" Each Christmas, at this time, my beloved father broadcast a message to his people in all parts of the world. Today I am doing this to you, who are now my people. As he used to do, I am speaking to you from my own home, where I am spending Christmas with my family : and let me say at once how I hope that your children are enjoying themselves as much as mine are on a day which is especially the children's festival, kept in honour of the Child born at Bethlehem nearly 2,000 years ago.

Most of you to whom I am speaking will be in your own homes, but I have a special thought for those who are serving their country in distant lands far from their families. Wherever you are, either at home or away, in snow or in sunshine, I give you my affectionate greetings, with every good wish for Christmas and the New Year.

At Christmas our thoughts are always full of our homes and our families. This is the day when members of the same family try to come together, or if separated by distance or events meet in spirit and affection by exchanging greetings. But we belong, you and I, to a far larger family. We belong, all of us, to the British Commonwealth and Empire, that immense union of nations, with their homes set in all the four corners of the earth. Like our own families, it can be a great power for good—a force which I believe can be of immeasurable benefit to all humanity. My father and my grandfather before him worked all their lives to unite our peoples ever more closely, and to maintain its ideals which were so near to their hearts. I shall strive to carry on their work.

Already you have given me strength to do so, for, since my accession ten months ago, your loyalty and affection have been an immense support and encouragement. I want to take this Christmas Day, my first opportunity, to thank you with all my heart.

Many grave problems and difficulties confront us all, but with a new faith in the old and splendid beliefs given us by our forefathers, and the strength to venture beyond the safeties of the past, I know we shall be worthy of our duty.

Above all, we must keep alive that courageous spirit of adventure that is the finest quality of youth : and by youth I do not just mean those who are young in years ; I mean, too, all those who are young in heart, no matter how old they may be. That spirit still flourishes in this old country and in all the younger countries of our Commonwealth.

On this broad foundation let us set out to build a truer knowledge of ourselves and our fellow men, to work for tolerance and understanding among the nations, and to use the tremendous forces of science and learning for the betterment of man's lot upon this earth. If we can do these three things with courage, with generosity and with humility, then surely we shall achieve that ' peace on earth, good will toward men ' which is the eternal message of Christmas, and the desire of us all.

At my Coronation next June I shall dedicate myself anew to your service. I shall do so in the presence of a great congregation, drawn from every part of the Commonwealth and Empire, while millions outside Westminster Abbey will hear the promises and the prayers being offered up within its walls, and see much of the ancient ceremony in which kings and queens before me have taken part through century upon century.

You will be keeping it as a holiday : but I want to ask you all, whatever your religion may be, to pray for me on that day—to pray that God may give me wisdom and strength to carry out the solemn promises I shall be making, and that I may faithfully serve Him, and you, all the days of my life.

May God bless and guide you all through the coming year."

Photo : Studio Lisa

The fifteen-years-old Princess framed in the blossoms of Philadelphus in the gardens of Royal Lodge, Windsor, in July 1941.

The young Princesses return from Spring gardening at Royal Lodge in April 1940.

The Path of Sovereignty

As the great day of the Coronation approaches, it is easy to forget that this magnificent ceremony is only the prelude to a lifetime's work, or rather a single brilliant incident in a task long ago begun but now assumed in full.

Seeing only the splendours that surround a throne, it is easy to imagine kingship as a pleasurable and desirable thing carrying with it an automatic exemption from all hardship and anxiety. In the past there have undoubtedly been Sovereigns who took this view of their position, just as there are always men in every walk of life who think only of their rights never of their duties. But in this country, during the last hundred years, we have been particularly fortunate in a succession of Kings and Queens who have, in the things that mattered most, invariably put duty before self.

During the centuries of our history, ideas of kingship have changed greatly and today it is no longer the Sovereign in person who draws up the laws, leads the armies or punishes wrongdoers. Yet as the direct power of our Kings and Queens has decreased, so their real power has become ever greater. In the long run it is not what people possess, either in wealth or power, that is of primary importance, but what they *are*. What our English Sovereigns have contrived to make themselves in the last hundred years is a combination of master and servant to their peoples. They rule as the focus of a Commonwealth's loyalty, but they serve as individuals dedicated to a mission.

From her earliest days Queen Elizabeth II has lived among people conscious of this mission. Her grandfather, King George V, was a great constitutional monarch who never spared himself in working for the common good: her father, King George VI, paid the price for similar efforts in a tragically early death. The consorts of both these

Kings are still, happily, able to carry on their untiring efforts for the good of the country, and we have seen recently in the Duchess of Kent's tour of Malaya yet another example of the readiness of all members of this great family to undergo danger or discomfort where the cause demands it.

With such a background the Queen's future might well seem assured, yet she has other gifts as great or greater than this. Those amongst whom she has lived have taught her her duties by their example, but it is by their affection, by their solidarity as a family, that they have taught her to be a balanced, happy and wise person.

For a Prince or a Princess who may one day rule a great country there is so much to learn that it is easy for the human values to suffer and the simple virtues to be forgotten. Only amongst people with a deep religious sense of the fundamental value of every man can magnificence and dignity go hand in hand with humanity and simplicity.

The family is older than kingship and private virtue than statesmanship. It is our Queen's good fortune to have been the daughter of a good man before she was the daughter of a great King.

As a child the Queen was mercifully free from the constricting life of palace ceremonial and could indulge in all the normal pursuits and pleasures of her age. Both her father and mother were people happier in the country than in town and happier outdoors than in. From them she early acquired her love of the countryside and, what so frequently goes with it, a love of animals.

Pretentiousness does not get far with a playful corgi and it needs courage to ride a pony at a fence. The British love of sport, so long as it is not only a matter of watching but of doing, may be no bad training for the rigours of kingship, and those who love to play hard more often than not work hard also.

Photo : Marcus Adams

A study of the Queen at the age of three years.

Rarely in their informal childhood photographs did the Princesses appear without their dogs. This photograph was taken when Her Majesty was ten years old in the grounds of Royal Lodge, Windsor.

But though the Queen loved solitude and the country, she was also encouraged to mix with those of her own age and soon showed a liking for parties—particularly those involving " dressing-up " or any sort of theatricals. No doubt her devotion to her sister and the informal friendliness of her parents' entertaining helped to make her contact with the outside world the easy and natural matter it has always remained. Early too was her introduction to the idea of the common-weal when lessons were backed up by such practical activities as Guiding and re-inforced by her father's well-known interest in boys' camps and similar activities.

Always for Queen Elizabeth work and play have gone hand in hand and her interests have constantly expanded. Before the war she learned tennis for her amusement. During the war she learned, in the ranks of the A.T.S., to drive army vehicles, a feat that gave her quite equal amuse-ment though it was achieved for the most serious of purposes. Later still, as a married woman, she was to take up sailing with her husband, a sailor

Prince, thus continuing in the tradition of her grandfather, one of the finest helmsmen of his day in the Royal Yacht " Britannia ". To her husband she owes also a greatly increased interest, as a spectator, in many games, notably those such as cricket and polo in which he takes a prominent part. Finally, from almost all her family back to King Edward VII, and from her own pleasure in riding, she derives a keen interest in horse-racing, the traditional " Sport of Kings ".

Many of these pastimes will now have to be drastically curtailed to fit into the crowded schedule of a reigning Sovereign, but the well-balanced outlook they have fostered is a gift that will always remain. And now will be shown the full worth of the other side of Queen Elizabeth's life, the preparation for her duties, as Sovereign, begun at the age of eleven and carried on un-ceasingly ever since.

From childhood the Queen's role has been marked out for her. Even before her father came to the throne her position as second in succession made it imperative that she should be trained to rule.

A keen horsewoman, the Princess Elizabeth is shown rewarding her pony after a victory at the Windsor Horse Show in 1944.

Photo : Dorothy Wilding

A Princess to charm all hearts.   The Princess was twenty when this photograph was taken.

In one of his rare moments of leisure during the tour of South Africa in 1947 the late King relaxes in a garden in the Natal National Park. Princess Elizabeth is an amused spectator.

She has been a willing and able pupil.

The wide interests that enable her to find something in common with all those her duties call on her to meet ; the memory to absorb and the self-possession to perform unaffectedly yet with dignity the endless ceremonies and rituals of which her official life is composed, such things call for long and arduous training. The self-discipline needed to live for hours each day in public, the constant sacrifices demanded of the wife and the mother by the Queen, these are not achieved without effort. At all times the Sovereign is entrusted with that most terrifying power, the ability to destroy in a moment those fundamental things that can only be created by years of effort, confidence between nations and peoples, confidence in the ultimate recognition of what is good and the ultimate condemnation of what is evil, confidence in the security and continuity of sound institutions.

The Sovereign is the focal point of loyalty, justice, mercy, integrity ; the Sovereign's example may elevate if it is good, it can hardly fail to corrupt if it is bad. The Queen must be at all times what her subjects at their best seek to be.

A hundred and fifty years ago such a description of a Queen's duties might have seemed merely Utopian. Today, with swift transport to increase the number of her subjects the Queen can see, and with the cinema and television to increase almost without limit the number of her subjects who can see her, this ideal standard in our ruler is a simple necessity if her tremendous task is to be rightly performed.

She will not fail.

———

Constitutional History, French, English Literature, these are some of the subjects in which she has had to make herself proficient, for she alone in Government must know how to stand above party or faction, she alone is able to confer the final honour our country can give in receiving foreign rulers and their representatives or welcoming its own most gifted sons. But her work has never been to her a separate thing from her personal life; it has both enriched her and been enriched by her. The childhood interest in Guiding has been maintained and widened with the passing years; her experience of motherhood has led to an active interest in the care of other mothers and of their children. Yet, though the Queen's day is devoted to the needs of her people, her Prime Minister is, rightly, expected to alter his schedule of visits to the Palace so as to allow the mother time to play with her children before they go to bed.

How much there is for her to do, despatches and memoranda to be read and mastered, festivals to be visited, occasions to be graced, heroes to be rewarded, disasters to be mitigated by her presence, and in all this no one can effectively deputise for the Queen. As head of the two National Churches of England and Scotland she has huge responsibilities, as head of the Armed Forces a host of unavoidable commitments. Well might she speak the words that Shakespeare puts into the mouth of King Henry V :—

—I know
'Tis not the balm, the sceptre, and the ball,
The sword, the mace, the crown imperial,
The intertissued robe of gold and pearl,
The farced title running 'fore the king,
The throne he sits on, nor the tide of pomp
That beats upon the high shore of this world,
No, not all these, thrice-gorgeous ceremony,
Not all these, laid in bed majestical,
Can sleep so soundly as the wretched slave,
Who, with a body fill'd, and vacant mind,
Gets him to rest—

The things that will support the Queen in her task are things familiar to all of us, a father's example, a husband's love, the affection of children, a sense of duty, belief in God. And, like her great namesake, Queen Elizabeth I, she can truly say :

" I have always so behaved myself that under God I have placed my chiefest strength and safeguard in the loyal hearts and good will of my subjects."

May we always be deserving of such trust and worthy of such devotion. God save the Queen !

A happy study of Her Majesty and the Duke of Edinburgh at the time of their betrothal in July 1947.

Shortly after their betrothal the Princess and the then Lieutenant Mountbatten accompany His Late Majesty King George VI on an inspection of the Home Fleet in the Clyde. They are seen here on board H.M.S. Maidstone.

ROYAL WEDDING.

On 20th November 1947 H.R.H. the Princess Elizabeth was married to H.R.H. the Duke of Edinburgh. They are seen (above) leaving Westminster Abbey after the ceremony and (below) on the balcony of Buckingham Palace.

Her Royal Highness in her bridal gown.

41

During a visit to Edinburgh in March 1949. The Princess chats with a Scots Sergeant-Major in full regimentals.

At Bangor in April 1949 the Duke of Edinburgh was installed as Chancellor of the University of Wales. He then conferred upon the Princess the degree of Doctor of Music.

Wearing a dark blue habit and the badges of rank of a Colonel of the Grenadier Guards, Princess Elizabeth rides with the Duke of Gloucester at the ceremony of Trooping the Colour, June 1949.

A birthday picture of Prince Charles who was one year old on 14th November 1949.

Princess Elizabeth and Princess Margaret at Aintree in November 1949. They had been watching Princess Elizabeth's horse Monaveen lose to Freebooter in the Grand Sefton Stakes.

In November 1949 the Princess flew to Malta to join her husband for a short holiday interspersed with official occasions.

At the Cenotaph on Remembrance Sunday, November, 1949.   Attendance at this annual service is a Royal duty which is most carefully observed.

Princess Margaret at the Spring show of the Incorporated Society of London Fashion Designers, March 1951.

The famous Canadian photographer Karsh of Ottawa was commissioned to take this portrait study of their Royal Highnesses Princess Elizabeth and the Duke of Edinburgh with Prince Charles. The photograph was taken in August 1951 when Prince Charles was 2¾ years old.

A charming portrait of H.R.H. the Princess Elizabeth taken at Buckingham Palace in July 1946.

Photo : C.O.I.

During the war the Princess served with the A.T.S.   She is seen here at the A.T.S. Motor Training Centre
where she received a month's training.

1951 *was Festival Year in Britain. The picture shows the King and Queen en route to St. Paul's for the service of dedication. The following day the Royal party visited South Bank and toured the Festival Exhibition.*

Prince Charles in confidential conversation with his grandfather. This photograph was taken on the Prince's third birthday, 14th November 1951.

Photo : Planet News

Against a background of mountains King George VI is photographed with his daughters in the National Park of Natal during the tour of South Africa in 1947.

A photograph of Her Majesty the Queen and H.R.H. the Duke of Edinburgh taken by Baron at Clarence House in December 1951.

Royal Ascot.   The Queen and Princess Elizabeth in the carriage procession, June 1951.

The service at St. Paul's to honour twenty-eight thousand American servicemen who, when based in this country, died in the War.   The picture shows the Queen, the Queen Mother and members of the Royal Family with members of the Government and Opposition.   The new President of the U.S.A., General Eisenhower, is sitting on the other side of the aisle from the Queen Mother.

56

Princess Elizabeth received a charming welcome from children when she visited Hastings in May 1951.

THE CHRISTENING OF PRINCE CHARLES

Four generations of the Royal Family. A photograph by Baron taken on the occasion of the christening of Prince Charles in December 1948.

His Royal Highness Prince Charles Philip Arthur George, heir apparent to the Throne.

His late Majesty while convalescing at Sandringham entertains a party of blind people from Felixstowe, July 1951.

In July 1951, Princess Elizabeth inspected Empire scouts on their way to the World Jamboree.   She is here shown walking with the Chief Scout, Lord Rowallan.

Photo : Baron

THE CHRISTENING OF PRINCESS ANNE

The Royal parents are photographed with the infant Princess in the White Drawing Room of Buckingham Palace, 21st October 1950.

Princess Anne's sponsors include (standing) Earl Mountbatten, H.R.H. Princess Margarita of Hohenloe-Langenburgh, the Hon. Andrew Elphinstone, (sitting) H.R.H. Princess Alice, Countess of Athlone.

Family photographs taken at Clarence House just before Princess Anne's birthday. The Princess on this occasion had little desire to be in the centre of the picture ; she preferred to explore the mysteries of the flower border.

Princess Elizabeth and the Duke of Edinburgh made a strenuous tour of Canada in October 1951. During their visit they travelled from coast to coast by train right across the country, stopping frequently to meet delegations and to attend functions in their honour. In populous districts the route was lined by cheering crowds; in the remote areas small groups of people, who had come many miles, waited to watch the Royal train go by. The Royal couple joined in many activities which are traditionally Canadian, including square-dancing. In the photograph above they are shown at a rodeo in Calgary, heart of Canada's cattle country.

Recalled from her tour of Kenya, Ceylon and Australia by news of the King's death Her Majesty Queen Elizabeth II is met at London Airport by her Ministers of State—7th February 1952.

Whereas it hath pleased Almighty God to call to His Mercy our late Sovereign Lord King George the Sixth of Blessed and Glorious Memory by whose Decease the Crown is solely and rightfully come to the High and Mighty Princess Elizabeth Alexandra Mary; We, therefore, the Lords Spiritual and Temporal of this Realm, being here assisted with these of His late Majesty's Privy Council, with representatives of other members of the Commonwealth, with other Principal Gentlemen of Quality, with the Lord Mayor, Aldermen and Citizens of London, do now hereby with one voice and Consent of Tongue and Heart publish and proclaim that the High and Mighty Princess Elizabeth Alexandra Mary is now, by the Death of our late Sovereign of Happy Memory, become Queen Elizabeth the Second, by the Grace of God Queen of this Realm and of all Her other Realms and Territories, Head of the Commonwealth, Defender of the Faith, to whom Her lieges do acknowledge all Faith and constant Obedience, with hearty and humble Affection; beseeching God, by whom Kings and Queens do reign, to bless the Royal Princess Elizabeth the Second with long and happy years to reign over us.

The Proclamation 8th February 1952 (above) at Temple Bar; (below) at the Royal Exchange.

At the first Royal Ascot since her accession, Her Majesty and the Duke of Edinburgh acknowledge the cheers of the crowd as they drive up the course.

The Queen presents her colour to the R.A.F. Apprentices School at Halton. The school trains apprentices for subsequent service in the R.A.F. as skilled technicians.

A visit to Marcus Adams' studio is always the occasion for renewed study of the crystal watch with which the photographer beguiles the children who sit to him. Here Prince Charles explains its mysteries to his sister.

Photo : Studio Lisa

Prince Charles shows his mother how a glove puppet works. The picture was taken at Balmoral for Prince Charles' fourth birthday.

Preceded by the Sword of State, hand-in-hand with the Duke of Edinburgh, Her Majesty makes her way
the State Opening of Parliament on 4th November 1952. The picture was taken as the procession move

hrough the Palace of Westminster—the first time photography has been allowed within the building on such n occasion.

REMEMBRANCE SUNDAY

Her Majesty, dressed simply in black, attends the annual service at the Cenotaph for the first time as Sovereign. Behind her are the Duke of Edinburgh and the Duke of Gloucester. In the foreground Mr. Churchill and Mr. Attlee are recognisable.

The Queen is received as a guest at the wedding of Miss Patricia Buller and Commander Ashmore in October 1952.

Her Majesty with the Lord Mayor of Birmingham and the Lord Lieutenant of Radnorshire at the opening of the new dam at Claerwen, October 1952.

At Balmoral in September 1952 Her Majesty and the Duke of Edinburgh entertained King Feisal of Iraq as their guest.

The Queen returns to London after her holiday at Balmoral. As the train leaves Ballater she waves through the rain spotted window.

In the floodlit arena at Windsor Horse Show in July 1952 the Queen hands Miss Pat Moss the rosette for her victory in the Ladies versus Gentlemen Team Jumping Championship.

After a busy afternoon in Edinburgh on 25th June 1952 Her Majesty is photographed when about to return to Holyrood.

Her Majesty was staying at Sandringham when news was received of the disastrous floods. She immediately toured the flood areas on the Norfolk coast and is here seen visiting a rest centre for flood victims in King's Lynn. February 2nd, 1953.

On 9th February the Royal Family arrived back in London from their stay at Sandringham.   Her Majesty now faces a heavy programme of public engagements leading up to her Coronation in June.

The Queen and the Queen Mother in the horse-drawn carriage procession at Ascot in 1951. The procession approaches the Royal Enclosure by way of the finishing straight, past the grandstands and the cheering crowds lining the rails.

TROOPING THE COLOUR
H.R.H. the Princess Elizabeth with H.R.H. the Duke of Gloucester enters the forecourt of Buckingham Palace after the ceremony of 1949.

H.R.H. Princess Elizabeth at the ceremony of Trooping the Colour in June 1949.   Her habit is the colour of the undress uniform of a Guards officer.

Prince Charles at play in the garden of Clarence House, June 1951.

The Queen enters the ring carrying the red rosettes she will present to trophy winners at a Horse Show.

The Sovereign's Guard of the Coldstream Guards marching to St. James's Palace for guard mounting. During the summer the guards for Buckingham Palace and St. James's Palace are mounted daily in the forecourt of Buckingham Palace. Each day a different regiment provides the guard.

A happy picture of Her Majesty with her two children at Balmoral. The picture was taken by Studio Lisa for Prince Charles's fourth birthday.

Trooping The Colour

Visitors to London in June of Coronation Year will be able to enjoy this colourful ceremony which is performed annually on Horse Guards Parade in honour of the Queen's birthday.

Actually trooping the colour is only part of a magnificent display of military precision, colour and inspiring music played by massed bands. Her Majesty, seated on her horse, rides slowly through the ranks of the Guards of her Household Brigade. She returns to the saluting base where she receives the Royal Salute in a march past supremely impressive in its military splendour. The picture on the left shows Her Majesty taking the salute in June 1951 when she wore a habit modelled on the uniform of a Colonel of the Grenadiers. Above, the Guards salute Her Majesty as they march past in line.

A Royal Command photograph taken by Baron in July 1949.

Their Royal Highnesses being welcomed by the Mayor of Nairobi during their visit to Kenya in February 1952.

H.R.H. Princess Margaret in an informal study.

Her Majesty in the ring at the International Horse Show at White City in July 1951—Festival Year.

Her Majesty is received at the Royal Film Show at the Empire, Leicester Square in October 1952.

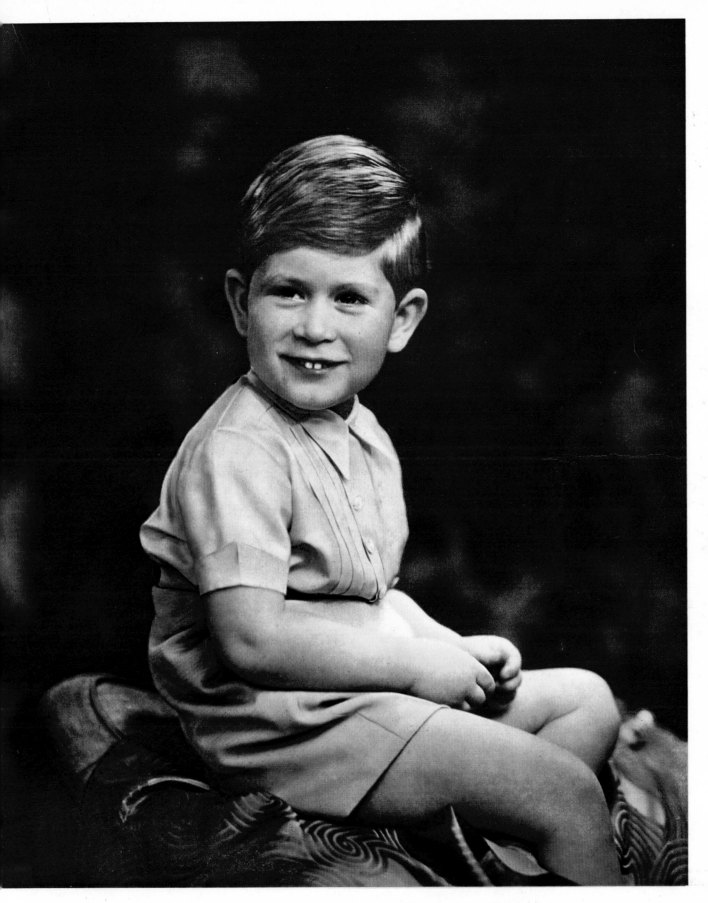

A photograph taken by Marcus Adams for Prince Charles' fourth birthday.

Mr. Douglas Chandor's portrait of Her Majesty the Queen. The picture is to be given by Mrs. Roosevelt to the British Embassy in Washington.

PRINTED IN GREAT BRITAIN BY L. T. A. ROBINSON LTD., LONDON, S.W.9

*Her Majesty Queen Elizabeth and His Royal Highness the Duke
of Edinburgh photographed after the State Opening of Parliament,
4th November, 1952.*